P9-DNA-880

BRARY

APR   2016

FAYETTEVILLE FREE LIBRARY

CLEAN SWEEP!

FRANK ZAMBONI'S
ICE MACHINE

Monica Kulling   *Illustrated by Renné Benoit*

TUNDRA BOOKS

For Barry, my hockey loving brother-in-law, and for Karen, who endures
M.K.

For my brother and my sisters
R.B.

Special thanks to Paula Coony and Richard Zamboni for reviewing the manuscript;
to Renné Benoit for her beautiful illustrations; to Sue Tate and Alison Morgan
for their kind support; and to Nancy Ennis, incomparable first reader.

Text Copyright © 2016 by Monica Kulling
Illustration Copyright © 2016 by Renné Benoit

Tundra Books, a division of Random House of Canada Limited, a
Penguin Random House Company

All rights reserved. The use of any part of this publication reproduced,
transmitted in any form or by any means, electronic, mechanical,
photocopying, recording, or otherwise, or stored in a retrieval system,
without the prior written consent of the publisher – or, in case of photocopying or other reprographic copying, a licence from the Canadian
Copyright Licensing Agency – is an infringement of the copyright law.

Library and Archives Canada Cataloguing in Publication

Kulling, Monica, 1952–, author
     Clean sweep! : Frank Zamboni's ice machine / by Monica
Kulling ; illustrated by Renné Benoit.

(Great idea series)
Issued in print and electronic formats.
ISBN 978-1-77049-795-5 (bound).–ISBN 978-1-77049-797-9 (epub)

     1. Zamboni, Frank J., 1901-1988–Juvenile literature.
2. Zamboni (Trademark)–Juvenile literature. 3. Skating rinks–
Equipment and supplies–Juvenile literature. 4. Inventors–United
States–Biography–Juvenile literature. I. Benoit, Renné, illustrator
II. Title. III. Series: Great idea series

GV852.K84 2016   688.7'691   C2015-900121-8
                                           C2015-900122-6

Published simultaneously in the United States of America by Tundra
Books of Northern New York, a division of Random House of Canada
Limited, a Penguin Random House Company

Library of Congress Control Number: 2015931500

Sources of inspiration:

Dregni, Eric. *Zamboni: The Coolest Machines on Ice.* Minnesota:
Voyageur Press, 2006.

Napier, Matt. *Z Is for Zamboni: A Hockey Alphabet.* Michigan:
Sleeping Bear Press, 2006.

Olson, Kay M. *Frank Zamboni and the Ice-Resurfacing Machine.*
Minnesota: Capstone Press, 2008.

Internet:

http://www.zamboni.com/

http://web.mit.edu/invent/iow/zamboni.html

http://inventors.about.com/od/xyzstartinventions/a/zamboni.htm

Edited by Sue Tate
Designed by Leah Springate
The artwork in this book was rendered in watercolor and colored
pencil on paper.
The text was set in Minion.
Printed and bound in China.

1 2 3 4 5   20 19 18 17 16

ZAMBONI and the configuration of the Zamboni® ice-resurfacing
machine are registered trademarks of Frank J. Zamboni & Co., Inc.

Bone Blades

In Switzerland
at the bottom of a lake
they found a pair of skates
made of animal bone
with leather straps
to tie the "blade" to the foot.

It was a way to get around
when ice was on the ground.

Later in Holland
they strapped on
wooden platforms
with runners attached
using poles to push
across frozen canals.

It was a way to get around
when ice was on the ground.

Invention made skates
lighter and safer.
Skating became
what it is today:
a way to fly around
when ice is on the ground.

Scritch! Scratch! Whoooosh! Skaters filled the Iceland Skating Rink in Paramount, California.

Frank Zamboni, his brother Lawrence, and their cousin Pete built the rink in 1939. When it opened in 1940, the rink didn't have a roof. By late spring, Frank put one on to keep out the California sun.

Skating at Iceland was a dream, except for one thing – the time it took to resurface the ice. The crew worked fast, but the job could take an hour and a half!

The first step was to make the surface of the ice level. A tractor dragged a planer that shaved down the pits and grooves. The crew then shoveled away the shavings, washed the surface, and sprayed on a layer of fresh water. Finally, they dragged a barrel of hot water around the rink to give the ice its gleaming finish.

Skaters waited and waited and grew tired of waiting. Frank decided to do something about it.

Frank Joseph Zamboni was born in 1901, in Eureka, Utah.

His parents had come to America from Italy to make a better life. Frank was their third child of four. When Frank was a baby, Mr. and Mrs. Zamboni bought a farm in Lava Hot Springs, Idaho.

As the years passed, Frank's father needed help on the farm. He took Frank out of high school when he was in ninth grade, and Frank soon proved to be clever at fixing trucks and tractors. In the early 1900s, children often left school to help their families.

California or Bust!

In 1920, Frank and Lawrence Zamboni moved to Clearwater, California, south of Los Angeles, to join their older brother, George.

George owned an auto repair shop. Frank and Lawrence got right to work, fixing cars and trucks. They were saving money to send one of them to trade school.

Frank studied electricity at the Coyne Electrical School of Chicago.

When Frank returned to California two years later, he and Lawrence opened the Zamboni Brothers Company. They did electrical work, drilled wells, and installed water pumps on dairy farms.

In 1923, Frank got married and was busier than ever. He and his wife, Norda, would have three children: Arlene, Jean, and Richard.

In 1927, Frank and Lawrence added an ice-making plant to their business. In those days, people placed blocks of ice in their iceboxes to keep their food cold. Packing plants used block ice to keep fruits and vegetables fresh, even when sending produce across the county by rail.

When people began to own refrigerators, Frank had an idea. "Let's use our ice-making equipment to build a skating rink."

"Skating rink? What do we know about skating?" asked Lawrence.

"Nothing," said Frank. "But we know how to make ice."

Frank had a problem. Most ice-rink surfaces rippled because of the pipes in the cement floor. These pipes, laid side by side, circulated the salt water that kept the floor cold enough to freeze the water that was sprayed on it.

Frank built a test floor using large, flat water tanks. When he finished making ice on top of it, he ran his hand across the surface. *No ripples!* The ice was as smooth as glass.

Frank built the Iceland skating rink using this method, but he didn't receive a patent for his rink floor idea until 1946. Thanks to Frank, Iceland had the smoothest ice for miles around.

Now Frank faced another challenge. Could he turn a 90-minute ice-resurfacing job for five men into a 10-minute job for just one?

Frank drew designs for a machine and built prototypes, or models.

Prototype No. 2 was constructed on a sled and towed by a tractor. But it didn't smooth the surface or pick up the shavings perfectly, so Frank went back to work.

Frank labored in a workshop behind Iceland. Sometimes folks stopped to ask what he was doing. When Frank told them, they often offered advice, such as, "It can't be done," or "Sounds crazy to me."

So Frank dug in his heels and tried harder.

But the Second World War came along and put a stop to Frank's work.

When the war ended, Frank was able to buy military parts, like an engine and axles, cheaply. He built his ice-resurfacing machine on the chassis, or base frame, of a Jeep.

It was 1949. Frank had spent nine years working on his invention. Now it was time to test it. *Would the machine work?*

Frank climbed into the driver's seat of the Model A.

"Start 'er up!" shouted Lawrence.

The blade on the Model A shaved the ice. The paddle and chain conveyor removed the shavings and dumped them into the holding tank on top. The machine then washed the surface, and finally, it applied fresh water using a towel to make the ice shine.

But the ride wasn't perfect. The four-wheel drive with four-wheel steering caused the machine to jam against the boards. When Frank switched to two-wheel steering, the problem was solved. The Model A cleaned the ice in one sweep around the rink!

Over the years, Frank would build many models, each one an improvement on the last. But, now, he needed a name for his company and his ice machine.

The towns of Clearwater and Hynes in California had merged to become the city of Paramount. Frank wanted to name his company the Paramount Engineering Company, but someone was already using that name.

Frank chose to use his own name instead. In time, folks came to think of Frank's amazing invention as a Zamboni machine.

In 1951, Sonja Henie, Norway's figure-skating superstar, bought two Zamboni ice-resurfacing machines. Henie had won gold medals three times in a row at the Olympics. Now she was making movies and performing ice shows.

Frank painted Henie's machines fire-engine red. That way the crowds could see the Zamboni machine do its work from wherever they were sitting. A rink was never the same once Frank Zamboni's ice machine had done its job!

Zippity Zamboni!

Fun facts abound when it comes to the popular Zamboni machine.

Did you know?

- The machine can remove up to 60 cubic feet of ice in one pass. That's enough shavings to make 3,661 snow cones!
- In 1960, it appeared for the first time at the Olympic Winter Games.
- In 2000, it was made into a token piece for the NHL version of Monopoly.
- In 2001, a Zamboni machine, with a top speed of nine miles an hour, was driven across Canada, from St. John's, Newfoundland, to Victoria, British Columbia, a trip that took four months.
- At the 2002 Olympic Winter Games in Salt Lake City, there were 20 Zamboni machines standing by to resurface the many ice rinks.
- In 2005 and 2013, McDonald's restaurants in Canada gave out mini machines with each Happy Meal.
- Zamboni machines are on every continent except Antarctica.